Theory Paper   Grade 8   2014   A

GW00498822

TOTAL MARKS
100

Duration 3 hours

Candidates should answer all FIVE questions.
Write your answers on this paper – no others will be accepted.
Answers must be written clearly and neatly – otherwise marks may be lost.

1   Complete the violin parts in the following extract adapted from a concerto grosso by
    Vivaldi, following the figuring shown under the basso continuo.

[15]

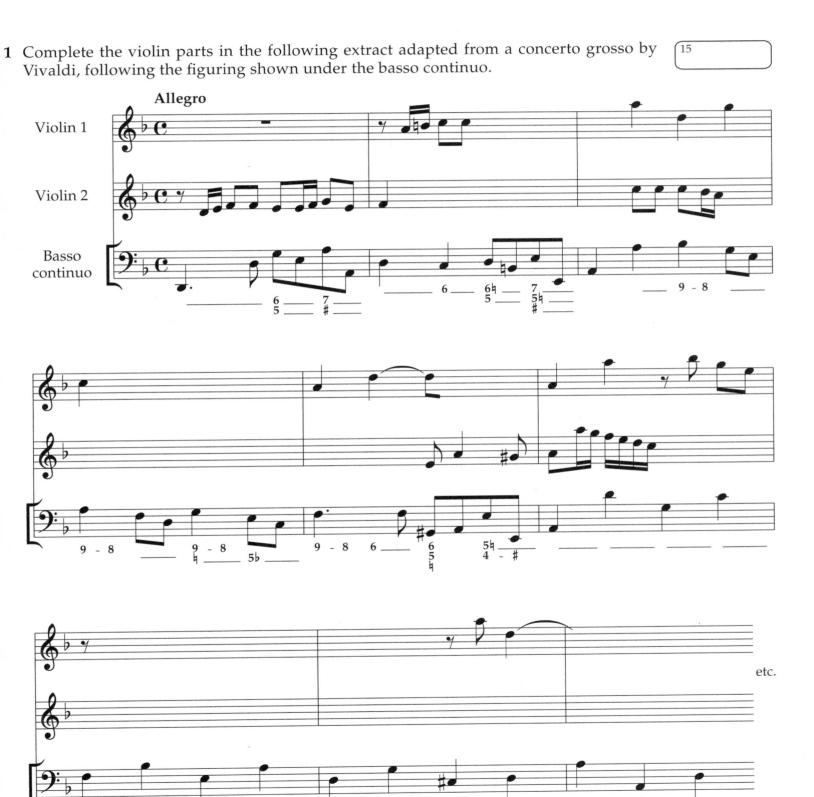

2 Complete the given outline of the following passage, adapted from a piano piece by Schumann (1810–1856).

15

3 Compose a complete melody of not less than 12 bars using **ONE** of the following openings and for the given unaccompanied instrument. Continue in the same style and include appropriate performance directions. Write the complete melody on the staves below.

HORN (at concert pitch)

OBOE

4 Look at the extract printed opposite, which is from a piano piece, and then answer the questions below.

(a) Give the meaning of:

con anima (bar 12) .... (2)

᠎ (e.g. bar 13) .... (2)

(b) Mark **clearly** on the score, using the appropriate capital letter for identification, one example of each of the following. Also give the bar number(s) of each of your answers. The first answer is given.

In bars 1–11

A an appoggiatura in the right-hand part (circle the note concerned).   Bar ....7....

B an acciaccatura (grace note) that forms the melodic interval of a minor second with the main note that follows it (circle the note concerned).   Bar .... (2)

C a diminished 7th chord in root position (circle the notes concerned).   Bar .... (2)

D a descending chromatic semitone (augmented unison) in the right-hand inner part (circle the notes concerned).   Bar .... (2)

E a melodic interval of a minor 2nd in the left-hand part (circle the notes concerned).   Bar(s) .... (2)

From bar 12 onwards

F a bar that is an exact repetition of the previous bar.   Bar .... (2)

(c) Identify the chords marked ∗ in bar 10 (shaded) and bar 18 by writing on the dotted lines below. Use either words or symbols. For each chord, indicate the position, show whether it is major, minor, augmented or diminished, and name the prevailing key in bar 10.

Bar 10 .... Key .... (4)

Bar 18 .... (3)

(d) Answer TRUE or FALSE to the following statement:

The harmonic intervals between the right-hand and left-hand parts on the last beat of bar 15 are all major 6ths.   .... (2)

(e) From the list below, underline the name of the most likely composer of this piece and give a reason for your choice.

        Haydn   Handel   Liszt   Stravinsky (1)

Reason:

.... (1)

5 Look at the extract printed on pages 9–10, which is from the first movement of   25
Tchaikovsky's *Manfred Symphony*, and then answer the questions below.

   (a) Give the meaning of:

      Timpani in H, Cis, E   ....   (3)

      a 2 (e.g. bar 1, flutes)   ....   (2)

   (b) Complete the following statements:

      (i)   On the first note of bar 5, the instruments that *sound* in unison with the first and third

         horns are the ...., the .... and

         the ....   (3)

      (ii) The first clarinet and first bassoon parts cross in bar ....   (2)

   (c) Using the blank staves at the foot of page 10, write out the parts as they would sound at concert
      pitch for:

      (i)   first and second horns in bars 6–7 (first note), using the given clef.   (3)

      (ii) first and second clarinets and bass clarinet in bar 7, using the given clefs.   (6)

   (d) Describe fully the numbered and bracketed harmonic intervals *sounding* between:

      1   first trombone and first trumpet, bar 5   ....   (2)

      2   second trombone and cor anglais, bar 7   ....   (2)

   (e) Answer TRUE or FALSE to the following statement:

      In bars 5–8, the second violins and violas play the same notes an octave apart.   ....   (2)

(c)   (i)

bars 6–7 (first note)

(c)   (ii)

bar 7

Theory Paper   Grade 8   2014   B

Duration 3 hours

Candidates should answer all FIVE questions.
Write your answers on this paper – no others will be accepted.
Answers must be written clearly and neatly – otherwise marks may be lost.

TOTAL MARKS
100

1   Complete the violin parts in the following extract adapted from a trio sonata by Corelli, following the figuring shown under the basso continuo.

15

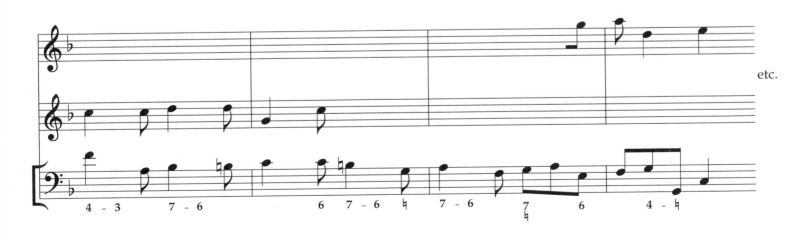

etc.

2 Complete the given outline of the following passage, adapted from a piano piece by Grieg (1843–1907).

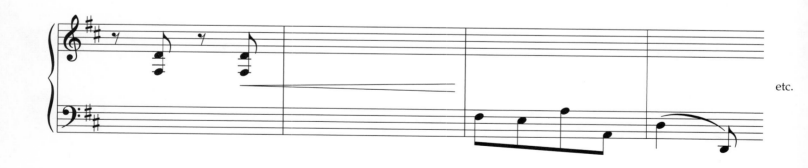

etc.

3 Compose a complete melody of not less than 12 bars using **ONE** of the following openings and for the given unaccompanied instrument. Continue in the same style and include appropriate performance directions. Write the complete melody on the staves below.

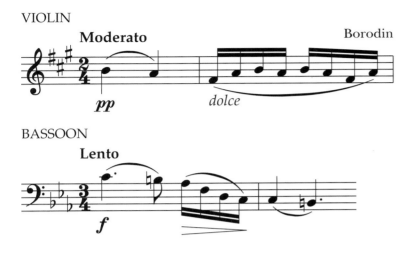

VIOLIN

BASSOON

4 Look at the extract printed opposite, which is from Mendelssohn's Violin Sonata Op. 4, and then answer the questions below.

25

(a) Identify the chords marked * in bars 3 and 8 by writing on the dotted lines below. Use either words or symbols. For each chord, indicate the position, show whether it is major, minor, augmented or diminished, and name the prevailing key.

Bar 3 .... Key .... (4)

Bar 8 .... Key .... (4)

(b) Write out in full the violin part of bar 13 as you think it should be played.

(3)

(c) Mark **clearly** on the score, using the appropriate capital letter for identification, one example of each of the following. Also give the bar number of each of your answers. The first answer is given.

In bars 1–10

A   a harmonic interval of an augmented 2nd in the
right-hand piano part (circle the notes concerned).   Bar ....7.....

B   a diminished 7th chord in the relative minor key (circle the notes concerned).   Bar .... (2)

From bar 11 onwards, in the right-hand piano part

C   a descending chromatic semitone
(augmented unison) (circle the notes concerned).   Bar .... (2)

D   a bar that contains three harmonic intervals of a major 3rd.   Bar .... (2)

(d) Name two features that suggest this extract is not the end of the piece.

1 .... (1)

2 .... (1)

(e) Complete the following statement:

IIIa corda (bar 10, violin) means .... (2)

(f) Give the full name (e.g. upper auxiliary note) of each of the following notes of melodic decoration in the violin part of bar 18:

X   .... (2)

Y   .... (2)

15

5 Look at the extract printed on pages 17–18, which is from Ravel's *Valses nobles et sentimentales*, and then answer the questions below.

(a) Give the meaning of:

   sur la touche (e.g. bar 1, violas)   .... (2)

   o (e.g. bar 2, harp)   .... (2)

   sourdines (e.g. bar 5, double basses)   .... (2)

(b) (i)   Write out the parts for clarinets in bars 5–6 as they would sound at concert pitch.

   Clarinets 1 / 2

(3)

   (ii)   Using the blank staves at the foot of page 18, write out the parts for horns in bars 9–10 as they would sound at concert pitch. (6)

(c) Mark **clearly** on the score, using the appropriate capital letter for identification, one example of each of the following. Also give the bar number of each of your answers. The first answer is given.

   From bar 7 onwards

   A   a bar in which the third and fourth horns play two consecutive harmonic intervals of an augmented 4th.   Bar ...12....

   B   a note and its enharmonic equivalent sounding at the same time between the second flute and harp parts (circle the notes concerned).   Bar .... (2)

   C   a major triad in first inversion *sounding* in three double-reed parts (circle the notes concerned).   Bar .... (2)

(d) Describe fully the numbered and bracketed harmonic intervals *sounding* between:

   1   upper note of violas and cor anglais, bar 4   .... (2)

   2   double basses and first bassoon, bar 6   .... (2)

   3   fourth horn and first clarinet, bar 12   .... (2)

(b) (ii)
bars 9–10

Horns

18

Theory Paper   Grade 8   2014   C

TOTAL MARKS
100

Duration 3 hours

Candidates should answer all FIVE questions.
Write your answers on this paper – no others will be accepted.
Answers must be written clearly and neatly – otherwise marks may be lost.

1 Complete the violin parts in the following extract adapted from a trio sonata by Corelli, following the figuring shown under the basso continuo.

15

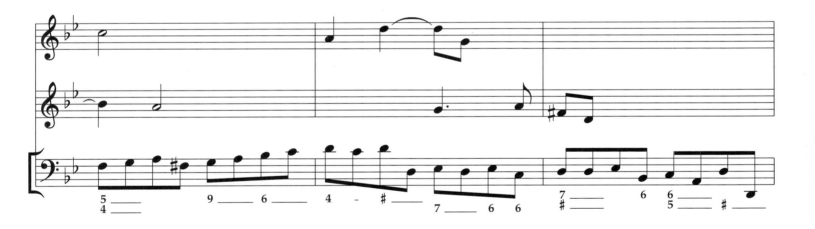

etc.

2 Complete the given outline of the following passage, adapted from a piano piece by Reinecke (1824–1910). Note that the left-hand part is in the treble clef.

Allegro moderato

3 Compose a complete melody of not less than 12 bars using **ONE** of the following openings and for the given unaccompanied instrument. Continue in the same style and include appropriate performance directions. Write the complete melody on the staves below.

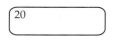

CELLO

FLUTE

4 Look at the extract printed opposite, which is from a keyboard piece, and then answer the questions below.

(a) Identify the chords marked ∗ in bar 9 (shaded) and bar 13 by writing on the dotted lines below. Use either words or symbols. For each chord, indicate the position, show whether it is major, minor, augmented or diminished, and name the prevailing key.

Bar 9 .... Key .... (4)

Bar 13 .... Key .... (4)

(b) Write out in full the right-hand part of bar 4 as you think it should be played.

(5)

(c) Mark **clearly** on the score, using the appropriate capital letter for identification, one example of each of the following. Also give the bar number of each of your answers. The first answer is given.

In bars 1–9

A   an unaccented passing note in the left-hand part (circle the note concerned).   Bar ....7.....

B   a harmonic interval of a compound augmented 5th between the right-hand and left-hand parts (circle the notes concerned).   Bar .... (2)

C   a perfect cadence in the relative major key.   Bar .... (2)

From bar 10 onwards

D   three successive melody notes in the right-hand part that form a Neapolitan 6th chord in the tonic key (circle the notes concerned).   Bar .... (2)

(d) Answer TRUE or FALSE to each of the following statements:

(i)   The music is made up entirely of regular four-bar phrases.   .... (2)

(ii)   The right-hand part of bar 3 is a repetition of bar 1 a major 2nd lower.   .... (2)

(e) From the list below, underline one period during which you think this piece was written and give a reason for your choice.

                1600–1700   1700–1800   1800–1900   (1)

Reason:

.... (1)

5 Look at the extract printed on pages 25–26, which is from the second movement of Bloch's *Concerto Symphonique*, and then answer the questions below.

(a) Give the meaning of:

8va ------------ (e.g. bars 1–2, first violins) .... (2)

div. (e.g. bar 2, cellos) .... (2)

a 2 (e.g. bar 5, clarinets) .... (2)

(b) Write out the parts for second clarinet and bass clarinet in bar 1 as they would sound at concert pitch and using the given clefs.

2nd clarinet (4)

Bass clarinet (2)

(c) Complete the following statements:

(i) On the first beat of bar 2, the lowest-sounding note is played by

the ...., the ....

and the .... (3)

(ii) On the first beat of bar 4, the instruments that *sound* an octave higher than the double basses

are the .... and the .... (2)

(d) Describe fully the numbered and bracketed harmonic intervals *sounding* between:

1 first horn and first oboe, bar 1 .... (2)

2 first violins and cor anglais, bar 3 .... (2)

3 first trumpet and second bassoon, bar 5 .... (2)

(e) Answer TRUE or FALSE to the following statement:

The violas are instructed to play triplet quavers in bar 1. .... (2)

25

Theory Paper   Grade 8   2014   S

Duration 3 hours

Candidates should answer all FIVE questions.
Write your answers on this paper – no others will be accepted.
Answers must be written clearly and neatly – otherwise marks may be lost.

TOTAL MARKS
100

1 Complete the flute parts in the following extract adapted from a trio sonata by Telemann, following the figuring shown under the basso continuo.

15

2 Complete the given outline of the following passage, adapted from a piano piece by Schubert (1797–1828).

15

3 Compose a complete melody of not less than 12 bars using **ONE** of the following openings  and for the given unaccompanied instrument. Continue in the same style and include appropriate performance directions. Write the complete melody on the staves below.

CLARINET (at concert pitch)

CELLO

etc.

4 Look at the extract printed opposite, which is from a piano piece, and then answer the questions below.
25

  (a) Name two similarities and two differences between bars 17–20 and 25–28.

      Similarities 1 ....   (1)

                  2 ....   (1)

      Differences 1 ....   (1)

                  2 ....   (1)

  (b) Write out in full the top line of the right-hand part of bar 20 as you think it should be played.

(3)

  (c) Identify the chords marked ✱ in bars 7 (shaded) and 17 by writing on the dotted lines below. Use either words or symbols. For each chord, indicate the position, show whether it is major, minor, augmented or diminished, and name the prevailing key.

      Bar 7 .... Key ....   (4)

      Bar 17 .... Key ....   (4)

  (d) Mark **clearly** on the score, using the appropriate capital letter for identification, one example of each of the following. Also give the bar number of each of your answers. The first answer is given.

     From bar 9 onwards

     A   arpeggiation in the left-hand part.   Bar ...20...

     B   a false (cross) relation between the right-hand and left-hand parts (circle the notes concerned).   Bar(s) ....   (2)

     C   an unaccented passing note in the right-hand part that forms the harmonic interval of a compound major 2nd with the bottom note of the left-hand part (circle the note concerned).   Bar ....   (2)

     D   a rising chromatic semitone (augmented unison) in the right-hand part (circle the notes concerned).   Bar ....   (2)

  (e) Answer TRUE or FALSE to the following statement:

     The largest melodic interval in bars 1–16 of the right-hand part is a major 9th.   ....   (2)

  (f) From the list below, underline the name of the most likely composer of this piece and give a reason for your choice.

            Haydn   Debussy   Chopin   Handel   (1)

     Reason:

     ....   (1)

5 Look at the extract printed on pages 33–34, which is from the first movement of Tippett's Symphony No. 1, and then answer the questions below. [25]

(a) Give the meaning of **pochissimo allargando** (bar 2).

.... (2)

(b) (i) Write out the part for first clarinet in bars 3–4 as it would sound at concert pitch.

Clarinet 1

(3)

(ii) Using the blank stave at the foot of page 34, write out the parts for third and fourth horns in bars 8–9 as they would sound at concert pitch, and using the given clef. (2)

(c) Describe fully the numbered and bracketed harmonic intervals *sounding* between:

1 second trombone and second horn, bar 5 .... (2)

2 cellos and first bassoon, bar 6 .... (2)

3 first violins and first horn, bar 7 .... (2)

(d) Complete the following statements:

(i) On the first beat of bar 2, the instruments *sounding* at the same pitch as the cellos are the

...., the .... and the .... (3)

(ii) A standard orchestral section not playing in this extract is the .... section. (2)

(iii) There is an instruction for an up-bow to be used by a string section in bar .... (1)

(e) Answer TRUE or FALSE to each of the following statements:

(i) In bar 1, the third flute and the second horn *sound* an octave apart. .... (2)

(ii) The first trumpet and the first trombone
sound an octave apart throughout the extract. .... (2)

(iii) The first note of bar 1 is the only place where every
brass instrument in the extract plays at the same time. .... (2)

(b)　(ii)
Bars 8–9

Horns